SO LONG

SO LONG

POEMS

JEN LEVITT

FOUR WAY BOOKS
TRIBECA

Library of Congress Cataloging-in-Publication Data
Names: Levitt, Jen, author.
Title: So long / Jen Levitt.
Description: New York : Four Way Books, [2023] | Summary: "Jen Levitt - So Long, Four
Way Books"—Provided by publisher.
Identifiers: LCCN 2022033096 (print) | LCCN 2022033097 (ebook) | ISBN
9781954245501 (paperback) | ISBN 9781954245518 (epub)
Subjects: LCGFT: Poetry.
Classification: LCC PS3612.E9345 S6 2023 (print) | LCC PS3612.E9345
(ebook) | DDC 811/.6—dc23/eng/20220722
LC record available at https://lccn.loc.gov/2022033096
LC ebook record available at https://lccn.loc.gov/2022033097

This book is manufactured in the United States of America and printed on acid-free paper.

Four Way Books is a not-for-profit literary press. We are grateful for the assistance
we receive from individual donors, public arts agencies, and private foundations
including the NEA, NEA Cares, Literary Arts Emergency Fund, and the
New York State Council on the Arts, a state agency.

We are a proud member of the Community of Literary Magazines and Presses.

for my family, especially my father—

CONTENTS

Notes

It hurts just as much as it is worth.

—Zadie Smith, "Joy"

AFTER

At first, it was like trying to live
in a human-sized aquarium, with everyone
watching me come up for air.

Then, it was like how the geese
wandered around that soccer field all Sunday
shitting everywhere, unconcerned with aesthetics.

Now, it's like people on the subway
most mornings, who mutter into their coffee,
Look at me—I'm right here.

1.

SOME DAYS I'D RATHER BE ANYONE ELSE

today it's the boy on the train
in a royal blue wind-
breaker & tennis shoes
tapping his foot
to whatever breezy melody
loose-limbed like a cross-country champ
& quiet as a nail
part of me will always envy
a faded button-down
full of possibility
how the light before dusk
borders a boy
I prefer the boy half
of the catalogue
the boy half of my body
the way my chest would look
without breasts
show me a hero
sandwich piled with meats
a boy's confidence
like adult teeth
how a boy doesn't need
to glance behind him at night
since he cultivates
a smile with wingspan
I've spent too much of my life
extracting loose hair from the drain
re-reading every text

I've ever sent
worried about excess
& the right way to ask for more
no woman I know isn't trying
to make of her body
something better
a blade sharp or weightless
while deep in the woods
a boy who has worked all day
sleeps under stars
devoted to nothingness
& the rain about to fall

ONCE I WAS IN LOVE

with all my friends   & sometimes still am
even though you can't say that out loud
except in a karaoke song   at a dive bar on the LES

I hate to swim but love the ocean
all that artificial   blue for miles
I miss my mother (who isn't dead) & always will

her illegible cursive on my refrigerator door
when we go shopping   she sits in the fitting room
while I try on bras & dresses for a wedding

I never learned how to sew   I don't know
the number of any doctor   who will I call in a winter
without her   I will never pick up the phone

MOST LIKELY

School nights I sat at a dimly lit desk
copying math problems onto graph paper
while a wooden bird with notched

wings I'd carved at summer camp
peered down stoically from its perch.
Across the cul-de-sac a man in his fifties

trained a Great Dane with a muzzle
& metal pole & a few college kids
listened to music or set off fireworks

we only heard the echoes of. In the car
my mother played *The Big Chill*
soundtrack & songs where women left

cruel marriages or swore off love,
which to me meant talking to your boyfriend
after midnight on a cordless phone.

All the desires I couldn't name
burned in my chest until they wilted
into entries about each girl in history

class or on my soccer team I "admired"
& "wanted to be friends with," preserved
in notebooks I still won't read. I had

no models. Instead, I sent inscrutable
emails, hid behind flannel, waited
for the world inside my mind or else

the larger, outside one, to loosen…
Now, every day I stand at the door
as the teenage girls—& those who aren't

girls—link hands, lead each other
down the halls as openly as water passing
through a clear container, & every day

I envy them, their ease, the words they have.
When they name their griefs & joys,
when they come out or go back in, grope

for something more & sometimes reach it,
they're me & not me. In my high school
yearbook, I was voted "most likely to

stay the same" & it's true, I'm still working
on my mind to accept my body, my poems
to look back without shame. In their essays,

the students wish these years could last
forever—even driver's ed, even Calculus—
even if or because nothing's happened yet.

IN THERAPY I MAKE INCREMENTAL PROGRESS

But what if I could skip a few stages & wake up
somewhere new—a dairy farm in Vermont?
A vacation, that would be nice! To discover
how to melt in the sun without putting any effort in.

As it is my knowledge amounts to tallies
on graph paper. Small computations. Quadrants of feelings
& behavioral tics. When I should just swallow a pill
& get over it. Sometimes I try to go low,

admiring trashcans, sidewalks, even doorstops
for all they hold upright & open. While I keep it all in.
A closet. Or the track where the high-school team
laps me in their sweat-resistant fabrics,

going nowhere. They look so natural in their tank tops,
those dutiful kids trying to beat time.

INTIMACY

On the morning of the new Q train, we passed
a woman's body slumped against a wall.
White liquid poured from her mouth like snow,

until the paramedics showed up, for which
everyone was grateful. In my mind I was busy
riding a Palomino through a forest, solving

an equation in air. My thoughts hard & soft,
a terrain. All week I wanted to talk to you
about this small sad thing, the woman's purse

at her side, hands trembling like my horse
at the stream, while we looked & kept
walking, these details that make up a life

& could help you know me. All this time,
I wanted you to understand the emptying in me,
below the earth, where someone was singing.

OUR LANGUAGE LOVES TO SHOW OFF

its metaphors: the way tragedies bloom,
explosions rain down, grief wraps us

in its private embrace, a chokehold.
Even at the end, we had one perfect morning,

changing the similes in our poems
& trying new ones on, like the suit I had made

(my first) for a party we never attended.
I'm still not sure what went wrong,

exactly, except time passed between us
like a bruised piece of fruit no one wants

the last bite of. One of us always seemed
to be made of glass, shattering everywhere.

(When light hits a fragment it panics,
replicating itself.) We strained to be ourselves.

Now I know loss is the opposite of emptiness,
it's a view of the lake obscured by trees,

& I want back every night I didn't press
a hand to your throat or take you

in my mouth, out of shame or fear. I think
I was scared if I made too much noise

whatever intimacy we'd gathered & assembled
with no manual would spook or crash.

Were we an operating system? A bookshelf?
Any small animal that comes too close to touch?

MY BROTHER HAS A WIFE

but pre-braces he was an echo
an insect   flew down a black diamond
threw a party with our parents away

now he manages a team
conducts performance reviews   in his summer tan
cannonballs   into the public pool

I'm managing my performance
so when my brother   & his wife invite me for dinner
I scrape my plate of watermelon rinds

a night moon forms in the leaves
my brother will be having   his first kid soon
& I'll help him paint the nursery

INSIDE A GREEK TRAGEDY THERE'S NO NEED

for an unlimited MetroCard
or green juice cleanse
just a chorus chanting your name
when you walk into a room
the mood is moonlit & interior
you prepare monologues
on ethics & speak them
into your fan's whir
while in the corner
your archetypal parents
mumble about wasted youth
you don't need a therapist
only belief in an impossible cause
like the gods you suffer
from pride not shame
walk for hours
in casual loose-fitting
summer-wear & arrive
at a fork where you must choose
between justice & mercy
as rock cliffs slope
down to an agitated sea
where your prophecies precede you
you can weep openly
as boats on the horizon
circling a shore though you may
have to turn into a tree
or constellation

because some minor hero
can't control his arrows
there is no selfhood here
but selfishness
remains & hunger
a robin's chicks in the eaves
call out to be fed
also heartbreak
you can't stop it
these flashes of light
in the orchard & amphitheater
or the olive grove
on a summer night
in this ancient life

SOME FLOWERS

In this version we're both better.
You've learned techniques

for cultivating stillness,
& I'm not afraid to touch you

in public. Each night's sleep
unfastens easily, each early morning

coffee keeps its heat for miles.
Even our failures collect

themselves as quietly as snow,
then melt in spring, so we can

try again. Some flowers
I don't know the name of bloom,

little nothings on our tongues,
like hunger. At the river

where a few boats consider a bridge,
our questions, small mirrors,

hold us up to ourselves, & every
walk sign promises more time.

NO ONE'S LOOKING

Lately waking at an indeterminate hour,
I know no one's looking for me.

I could walk across a bridge & back
or burrow in, king of my oscillating

fan. Minutes sag like low branches
in snow. I'm taking my adulthood slow,

like medicine. Arranging flowers in a vase
is something nice to do for yourself,

that color rush, serotonin spike, even if
they won't survive the week. The cut stems

stripped of function, the smaller griefs
in that. Like how my niece at night stands

in her crib refusing sleep, eyelids fluttering
open, closed. Soon, all the world's

nieces will be old enough to want another
earth, a second chance, as we warm

by degrees. We're at a boil now, over-
flowing with want. These are trying times.

But time's trying, asking us to stay awhile
longer inside the length of this moment.

IF

when I held it up to the light
it was more holes than shirt, more string
than kite, more tonic than gin

when I bit down, it turned tasteless
& soft, a laundered sock

when viewed from a distance
it was a drop of water in a lake,
a lake but not the water in it, a painting

of a lake in winter with snow covering it
indistinguishable from a field

YESTERDAY I RODE THE TRAIN

out to where waves touch a shore
& like the water I've spent years
approaching & retreating   at the other end

kids I used to teach   now have kids
of their own   some are artists or officers
some never got through high school

three died   we cross paths like subway lines
& what we ask of each other
the future will decide   once in the park

we saw a hawk perched on a backboard
the day was windless   clouds overhead
tell me   which of our choices matter

SUPER BLOOM

for Mike Homolka

Mike, there's a new coffee shop
on the avenue
with young potted plants
construction noises
& kids wailing
my inner life in shambles
I know so little about so much
binary code
ancient civilizations
what happened to the neighborhood
temples & marketplace
now that we have the internet
to orbit around meaning
& never quite land
why is it so hard
to make ourselves happy
people I mean
with our unprecedented
personalities & devices
I know we're trying
after a red-eye we gather
around the baggage claim
to watch our belongings
fall out of a hole
in the ceiling or wall
but Mike, what if all we need
isn't microwaveable
noodles or noise-cancelling headphones

just a good bottle of red
some talk about teaching
a poem in our heads
for when you're waking in Spain
& I'm here in Yorkville
a distance merely physical
one fact among many
like Mike, did you know
ghost flowers bloom a few
weeks each year
under desert conditions
they don't produce
their own nectar but mimicry
attracts the bees
who pollinate them awhile
it's like when language finds us
& I reach out to you

2.

SO LONG

My father coughs into the phone again.
They're watching the *NewsHour*
or my mother is making dinner, or it's her voice
catching on the other end. Between us

a silence like the years collecting. What
will I do with her dishes & glass serving bowls,
his books, her linens & Joseph Cornell boxes?
Where to store the dozen sprained wrists,

dusky smells of summer & sports equipment
we have no use for? Childhood is like a sentence
I wrote then erased, adulthood like expired
fruit—or not-yet-ripe, depending on the day—

& after I put down the phone, I lie awake for hours
listening to a car alarm that won't stop ringing.

*

Inside the familiar hum of the Metro-North,
the sun in my eyes reminds me I'm most myself
in transit, with no other place or way to be.
I consider choosing between music & a novel,

then stare out the window for forty minutes,
undecided. At my parents' house,
my father nods off while reading, in glasses
I never knew he wore. My mother slips

outside to water her hydrangeas, & I sit with my wobbly
longing for the future, a feeling of family
like pulling on a thread, unspooling, intact.
Somewhere in the city, friends are making noise.

The sky gives nothing away. Tonight will be cloudy
or full of showers; tomorrow, sun for days.

*

M. & I talk intimately in a public place,
airing our small grievances with one another
like picking apart chicken on a plate.
The woman next to us interrupts to say

she appreciates our honesty, which she finds
rare in female friendship. What, exactly,
did she hear between the whir of espresso machines
& others' conversations? We're all misunderstood

most of the time & try not to make it legible.
At home later, I'll spend hours revising
words I spoke as though a melody's discernible.
Radio song too low to make out meaning.

Every night this week I've eaten alone
in my apartment looking through strangers' windows.

*

I don't know if this is a dream or a nightmare,
my father says on the car ride home. Green leaves
run on a loop like a movie reel, the Radio Shack's
closed, the Borders Books now a Trader Joe's,

the way their kitchen has become a pharmacy
of pills & drips & drugs, though they still walk
the winter beach, more slowly now, still watch
the Mets lose. When their reliever gives up

a homer, he goes to bed early, slippers shuffling
on hardwood. Unable to sleep, my mother
stays up late reading in his chair, says to no one,
Without him, I don't know how to live.

I imagine a family of deer foraging in the woods,
the blue-black dark where they feel most free.

*

All the diners we sit in after doctors' appointments:
City Limits, Elm Street, Bull's Head, Lakeside,
where outside our window booth a lethargic turtle
snaps at a piece of bread, then slides back into mud.

We order fries & chocolate shakes, or omelets
with meat & cheese, never salad, never tea,
my mother's usual substitutions—a side of tomato
slices, no potatoes—dissolved to acquiescence.

The silences, thick, cloudy, only amplify our habits.
My brother taps at his phone, my father shakes
his head, receding somewhere inside himself,
my mother offers sugared words we won't swallow.

All I'm good for lately is making lists: father, mother,
daughter, son. Family like the pit of an apricot or peach.

*

I'm rereading Roth to recognize my father,
what it was like to be Jewish in America in the second half
of the twentieth century: archery at Camp Mah-Kee-Nac,
buffet-style Bar Mitzvahs with cascades

of whitefish, sneaking the Dodgers on the radio
while conjugating French verbs. I didn't know his father
never went to college, took over his in-laws'
import business before the marriage fell apart.

Now, lying in bed after treatment, in the white quiet
of mid-afternoon, he says he wants to go to Winnipeg
to see his father's father's grave. *He had such
a hard life. I think I'll take your brother with me.*

Bunched socks on the carpet. *Well, what about me?*
A beat. *I hadn't thought of it. But yes, you come, too.*

*

The Sunday nights he'd drive me back to boarding school
I could barely breathe past Amenia I was so anxious
that whole first year. So he'd tell stories from his life
before kids—breaking an arm at summer camp, the Peace

Corps in Tanzania in the '60s, hours lost to back roads.
Now when I enter a room, it's *I'm glad you're here*
& *Where'd you go?* & at night, *Jen, talk to me* as if we haven't
spent all day together reading or watching *The Plot Against America*

a third time through. I love, though can't fully compute,
how he sees himself not in Herman, the steady patriarch,
but Alvin, the wayward cousin who joins a communist coup
to down the President's plane, ready to die for the Jews,

when his favorite advice, no matter the situation, is *You know
what John F. Kennedy said: When in doubt, do nothing.*

*

At the hospital, we take a ticket from the parking garage
but can't figure out where to insert it to pay.
The needle keeps falling out when he moves his arm.
The sour smell of sickness, like flowers in a vase too long.

We start a crossword, I ask him what *haimish* means,
but he's dozing. My mother scrolls through headlines on her phone.
Above us, someone's painted a skylight with acrylics—
treetops & cartoon clouds—adjacent, in a way, to serenity.

Walking out hours later, she asks him to button his shirt,
pick up his feet when he walks. He swats her away
but on the car ride home unleashes what he'd held—
You're a fucking bitch, his voice breaks, breathless.

After that, we move like insects caught under glass.
It's the season for harm—chill in the air, deceptive sun.

*

Early Sunday we're in the driveway
shoveling snow, & it's almost anachronistic
how we push these tools with plastic
handles I haven't held since childhood,

neither of us speaking, focusing our energy
on what we can change. There's a thrill
to the silence our work takes, our muscles aching
against this finite task & the fact of him

upstairs under blankets, still in the world.
In the basement later, next to shelves crammed
with art books & loose Monopoly money,
she drags an iron over linen napkins, his good shirt.

Overnight, the snow will turn to rain. Pain & beauty lie
so close, one is always taking the other's name.

*

On the subway platform late at night,
a woman holding a bouquet
offers me three white lilies—
I wonder how I must seem to her.

In my apartment, I fill a glass with water,
keep the flowers long after they wilt
to learn something about beauty & the will
it takes to stay alive.

Lately, mornings are all nerves.
Little snow islands in the park veil the grass,
though a few blades poke through.
I'm waiting for a feeling I can't yet name.

Somewhere north of here, the beach
is a million tiny shells coloring the sand pink.

*

An electric-blue light blankets the night sky over Manhattan.
For three or four minutes we thought apocalypse
(everyone on my block at their windows, speculating)
until we learned of the fire at a power plant in Queens.

Now I'm listening to the radio with the lights off,
to sirens outside, the low sounds of a plane overhead,
while my neighbor fights with someone
on the phone through the wall. All this noise

& below it, the frequencies I can't hear:
a bird on my fire escape swivels its head to locate food,
candle wicks reconstitute under thin flame,
moss breathes on trees & a few stars collapse.

My father, when he passes through—will he be within earshot
still, or somewhere farther out I can't gain access to?

*

On his birthday, we go to Flushing to watch the Mets.
I meet him at Grand Central & he's stooped, short of breath,
his MetroCard won't swipe, he doesn't get a seat
until we're a stop away. When we spot my brother,

his mood reverses: he eats sausage & peppers, cheese fries
with ketchup, vanilla soft-serve, & in between innings
watches videos of his granddaughter touching her head
on command, parading a plastic ball in a teacup until it drops.

The weather shifts from breeze to sun, my father cheers
for his favorite pitcher & boos the deadbeat slugger.
We pack up early to avoid the rain. I am not a son
but a daughter who will ride back with him on the 7 train

& put him on the Metro-North home to Stamford where
he just might take my mother out, he's feeling so fine.

*

There's his writing desk in the basement & the recliner
in the living room where he naps, the wicker placemats
he wipes clean of crumbs. Then his footsteps on the stairs,
which means he's coming up to say good morning.

On his bureau the leather wallet stuffed with receipts
& the baseball cap he's always losing. By the fireplace
a monogrammed briefcase he hasn't used in years,
what time accumulates. I know he's going to miss all this,

& the small conversations with strangers, the beach
in summer or winter while the Manhattan skyline
rises in the distance, evenings on the porch with my mother
reading the paper & watching the sun go down.

Forty-five years together is more than half their lives.
I got it wrong, above. It's we who will miss him in it.

*

In my childhood bedroom, going through papers,
I find a poem I wrote in college almost twenty years ago:
"The other team's won, but my father in his blue vest,
sunglasses safety-pinned where they've split, will listen

the whole ride home as I babble on about every detail
of the game, & he plays along, recreating all the possible
scenarios that could make me a hero. For a moment
I'm quiet, looking out at the window at the brightness

of the day, where suddenly I see him in his backyard
forty years ago, playing catch with Sass until the sun
goes down & his father appears, calling *Time to come in—
game called on account of darkness!* I turn then

to look at my father, who says *I am so proud of you*
& I won't know what that means until years later."

*

Dad, do you remember summers before the new millennium?
Every weekend we drove across the state for tournaments,
through towns I'll always recognize—Madison, Milford,
Hamden. I could have caught fly balls you hit all day

into night, could have listened to you list the year each song
on the radio came out, & where you were, but we have to keep
moving, toward the present, so I can show you something beautiful
a student wrote. She found a diary where her childhood-

self had asked, *When you read this, please remember me.*
I can't believe your hospital's so close that I can visit after work
& we can talk about our days, the news, the books
you still have in you, until you drift off into almost-sleep.

Soon, we'll have to find another way to meet, as moonlight
makes the river glow, & look at how lucky I've been, for so long.

3.

AUTOBIOGRAPHY

Is it enough that I tried to do no harm?
I drank the milk before it spoiled,

biked to work, held doors. When I crushed
the occasional spider, I felt mostly sorry.

In the city, nature was hard to follow,
incognito in crevices along the river,

but who can tell a flower from a weed?
I met the not-knowing, & it bloomed in me

like a seed. Traffic blinked, an organism,
while I trained my mind on the mind,

which took forever. I couldn't think my way
into the future, where love was a country

I'd never visited but wanted to. The ocean
repeated while we wandered the lemon groves.

WALK THROUGH

In *My Autobiography of Carson McCullers,*
a writer is searching McCullers' queer life

for clues about her own, like I'm searching
in both women's lives for clues about mine.

Can writing ourselves as we are create a door
for someone to walk through? Okay. I'm thirty-

something, white, a woman, gay, though there
were years I spent like an extra in a foreign film.

What is being *out* if no one hears you say it,
or if words don't exist for how you feel or you

don't know them—the words or the feelings—
yet, or if just saying the words & feeling them

don't mean anything without a story or proof,
or if moving looks the same as standing still?

You're on an ice floe as it melts & then you're
in the ocean anyway, wet, wishing you'd jumped,

& I wasted so much time like that, treading
water, afraid of *what?*—failing, desire?—

& I vow not to waste as much now (but do I
anyway, every minute I click through the internet?)

shrinking life to a thumb, stone on a beach,
mollusk, molecule, wringing the life from my life.

GO INWARD

It was for a friend's wedding that I found myself
back in temple with a lapsed hippie rabbi
who, in honor of the 50th anniversary
of his bar mitzvah, had decided to swap the traditional
prayers for songs from Broadway shows.
The capacity crowd shook noisemakers
& sang "Good Morning Starshine"
with a joy that surprised, then overtook me—
like a stadium wave when the home team scores—
second only to Rabbi Jonathan himself
explaining how in God's command to Abraham
to *go forth & found* a nation he noticed
the verb also means *go inward*, as in receiving
a stillness or sitting softly with oneself.
I thought of my father drowsy from chemo,
how we both needed this kind of attention,
a close reading, as would the country
a week later when at a synagogue in Pittsburgh
a man opened fire & thousands of Jews
& non-Jews returned to temple, in whatever
the opposite of an exodus is. When I was young,
I remember feeling faith privately, a direct line
to God, which the world or adulthood
diluted. Three times a year I'd sing along
with the cantor, not knowing what words meant.
That Saturday morning in temple, the leaves
changed & a congregation belted out Sondheim,
the country prepared to grieve, my father

coughed under covers, & I found in strangers
as much as in any book or prayer no promises
but, like hearing a rustle in deep woods & turning
to locate its source, the chance for something rare.

JOY

In the newest scan, the spots on my father's spine
lit up like moons. Erosion of bone,
our small lives inflamed. We watched an hour
of bad TV in the hospital room before I took a cab home.

This morning walking up Broadway,
I was surprised by my freedom, the width
of the city blocks. At breakfast, Catherine Barnett
quoted Marilynne Robinson who quotes

Dickinson happy in her solitude, for the chance
to know her *inner other*. Could it be thrilling
to find a different me inside of me,
like a stunt double or someone who speaks French?

All week my students catalogued their joys
& pleasures by way of Zadie Smith, disappointed
not to truly *know* joy, that desperate, painful bliss.
I had to remind them of the corollary—

so much can give us pleasure if we let it.
A father double-knots his daughter's laces
on the crosstown bus, I eat an apple I picked myself
with a balanced ratio of sweet to tart.

Now as I head south on Broadway, the sky's darkest blue
hangs on. Didion, sick of this city by thirty,

left. I have no place I'm supposed to be.
The leaves, before they fall, could last forever.

LIGHT WORK

The sun reflects onto a beige building
of strangers, where across from you a woman
is washing her windows with a cloth.

She stretches her arm to scrub the grate beyond the glass.
She's holding Windex in her other hand.
Until now, you've never considered your windows,

what it would take to make them shine.
It means putting in the work, your mother would say.
She would say a lot of things about upkeep

& neglect—she's hammered a nail over your bed,
threaded curtains through a metal rod, wanting so much
for you. But what is acceptable for you to want?

DAUGHTER

Yes, I've heard the story of my mother,
the ones she lost so I could be born,
those winter months in the N-ICU where
they visited me daily. Now I'm trying to live

a life apart, like I was taught, accumulating
socks, vacuuming dust. If I were good,
I'd visit on weekends so she could sleep
an extra hour or pull up weeds. I'd stand behind

him as he pushes the walker down the hall,
where she's taken up the rug so he won't trip.
I'd learn to change his apparatuses & when
he insists he's full, argue until he eats

another bite. But I don't. Because helping
to lift his legs or peel a boiled egg
only confirms what we've lost. The last
time I was home, she & I walked the winter beach

while the ducks bobbed above the waves
& an unknown virus was killing the racoons,
collapsing their nervous systems. At the edge
of the shore road, she spotted one, neither dead

nor living. *That's awful,* I said, *but don't get
too close.* I was looking at the sky or the water,

two kinds of blue, before I rode the train back
to my quiet life & became a stranger again.

THROW THE REST BACK

for Lizzie Harris

In a rare moment of clarity, we & the breeze
stood still. Ahead of us, a dog was going nuts
over a gull & I was holding your daughter,
who reached out to touch my ear, then a loose
strand of hair, until there was nothing left
on earth I didn't love. It was mid-summer
in our thirties. You'd waited years to welcome
this life made from your life, & I was busy
practicing unattachment, like a plastic bag
the wind frees. Our thirties, when we cradled
small flames, finally figured out taxes, quit jobs.
It was the summer my father would die
& I'd sit in the dark listening to his voicemails—
It's late, no need to call me back—letters
without a return address. Do we ever reach the end
of longing? Like fishing nets dropped underwater
for what we can't see. I still want a different
body, with angles & fewer curves, another hour
before bed—before he was sick, or sick
but not yet dying—to talk to him about our days,
how we spent them, what we saved & owe.
But more, I want to stop tending, like a mother,
my old shames—all the people I could have
been, in all the rooms, if words had left my mouth.
They cling to me when I try to set them down.
Or I catalogue their parts, dust & study them
for clues. That Sunday morning, we collected

shells & stones for skipping, a gray feather,
shards of sea glass, warped, translucent.
Later, I'd thread string around the best ones
& tie knots to make a mobile, throw the rest back.

NO BIRDS

It's true—sometimes, driving slowly on the highway
with the radio on & the sun looking in, I notice

as if for the first time my happiness. The not-wishing
for another timeline or turn. Like watching a live-

stream of birdfeeders on YouTube, how when two blue jays
& a stubborn oriole peck at seeds, I along with 356

others tune in from somewhere. Forget progress;
what about moments we pass through, like desire,

like pain? The goose on her rock at the lip of the pond
won't budge. She's guarding eggs. So, I sit with my

hunger, the hum of the dryer tumbling my shirts,
night's thin slice of moon. In a few weeks, five furred,

yolk-colored goslings will paddle, flanked by a parent
on each side. A matter of process, like those parts

of me getting wilder. When I check the livestream later,
no birds, but rain is falling. 84 others hear it, too.

JARDIN DU LUXEMBOURG

In the *Jardin du Luxembourg* I sat at the edge of a small,
peripheral garden. People moved their chairs close
hoping to catch the sun, & two gardeners shoveled earth
around a statue of a man. One wore blue gloves
& one pink, they spoke casually in a language
I didn't understand. One dug, one softened the soil
with a forked hoe. All around me people thought
their thoughts, like *I loved you but not how I wanted.*
When the gardeners paused to study their work,
a third man turned to admire the men covered in light,
one older, one young, who threw their shovels into the truck
& picked up shears. They started to trim the grass
around the statue then, so that it made a perfect circle,
the statue of Paul Verlaine, that destitute
Symbolist poet. I don't know more about him.
The admiring man stretched, the trees opened their leaves,
the denseness of the breeze was not unlike a collection
of hard feelings. Soon I would have to get up
& walk back into my life, where my jeans were too tight
& no one looked at me the way she did, once,
while the gardeners with their instruments went on
trying to make the earth around Paul Verlaine
beautiful, & the admiring man pedaled his bike away.

INTO SPRING

for Maya Popa

How did we get here, to this particular moment
when the world's finally returning, the buds
on the trees, a hint of sun? We know how much it took
to find our way back to ourselves, the loneliness
of months spent indoors, scratching out words
we wouldn't say or send, leaves rustling against the glass,
people we loved lost to circumstance, to history…
There are days I wish for us the ease of our early years,
the beginning of our lives in poetry, our lives
together—little moments in cabs or on the subway,
snacks in your kitchen, the fading winter light.
We're older now & maybe smarter, I'm not sure.
We're more aware of what the world does to us
in the name of progress, in the name of love.
I put things aside for love. I hollowed my insides
until I was a shell, & I shattered. We walked to the end
of the pier, looked down at the water & returned
with no souvenirs, just the taste of salt on our skin.
What can we do but write it down? There are days
I wish us younger & without knowledge—
no one will have died yet, no lovers slipped
through our lives' netting, no place will have locked
its doors. But mostly I wish to be sitting
near you again, at separate desks within earshot
of a copy machine, a song on a laptop, a window
through which light, the way we listened to our hurt,
the birds, the wind, & followed them into spring.

STILL LIFE

Once, in summer,
I drove past a row of rusted
mint-green lockers

sitting in a field, perfectly
intact. Could we ever
abandon our lives like that?

THREE DAYS BEFORE WHAT WOULD HAVE BEEN
YOUR EIGHTIETH BIRTHDAY

we throw a party for you & look—
can you see the defiant heads of dandelions
birdfeeders swaying in wind
some tall trees

the stone path
as it slopes into the woods
bits of quartz with their edges poking out
like little icebergs

Amaia & Hazel can climb
The Big Rock now
on the front lawn hand to hand up & up
when last time they needed a boost

Daddy, did you miss me
my niece to my brother
as he carries her down
legs wrapped around his waist

yellow forsythia separates
our house from the neighbor's
some showboating clouds
cross my line of vision

Dad, do you miss me
on the Metro-North & Major Deegan

the swept sky surrounding me
from all angles

on the Greenport ferry
waves collect & dissipate
over the edge
of the past

where you're waiting on the other side
in a ball cap & sunglasses
jeans you call dungarees
the car radio plays classical music

or a little jazz
some rich person's tennis court
rises on our left
& all the trees buzzing with summer

you squint at the camera
in a red polo shirt in 1995
my brother's smiling wide
light blondish hair on my legs

I've missed some cue
my eyes are closed
I'm still learning how to step inside
my life & just float

LETTER TO MY FATHER FROM PROVINCETOWN

I want to write down   something about this life
in case memory doesn't exist there

or writing doesn't   I came here alone & was afraid

                              I wasn't thinking of you yet
bees circled around flowers
most mornings a light-ish rain

                    *

it's funny to remember the summer you were here
wearing women's sunglasses
you bought from a gas station

                    after you'd lost your pair

in that non-place what does time sound like
& who will explain the electoral college to me

I know I can't call you there

                    but could another edge unfold

on this low rock at an intersection
in my life   I'm thinking of you now (is that enough?)

while a ribbon hangs from a post
with no particular purpose

except to amplify
orange in wind

*

tomorrow I'll go to the beach   if the weather holds
I might dip my feet in the water

like those weekends at the shore with the great-aunts
when you tried to teach us poker

we stacked our chips at the kitchen table

      into neat
      columns
      of primary
      colors

(I loved the satisfaction of clicking each one into place)

*

a wrist was always tapping
a cigarette into an ashtray   while an uncle worked the grill

at first we didn't understand high-low

                    but you explained the beauty
                      is sometimes even when you lose

you still win half the pot

DUNES

When I finally reached them, a young father
was trying to teach his daughter how to cast.
She flicked her wrist, overshot, found the motion
the second time around. I'd run four miles
to get here & didn't think I'd make it, then sat
awhile attempting to be still, to regard the teenagers
stripping down to their suits with recognition,
kindness, & not my usual judgment aimed inward.
Yesterday, an ecologist was explaining how
so much in nature forms from loss—take beaches,
he'd said, damage the desired state for a certain
kind of growth. On the walk home my feet hurt,
I came across a turtle in the road, flies attaching
to its split shell, & waited for someone else
to move it. Like how she'd told me I needed
to open, but how? I mean it literally: I can't figure
out the mechanics. Online another poet vows
not to *collude anymore with modes of despair.*
But what about the opposite, what it would mean
to shelter despair like a child or childhood pet?
This is me trying to make an opening. For some-
thing unformed to enter. A new kind of noticing.
The willingness to risk failure for the possibility
of love. On the dunes, a dark-haired woman walking
barefoot along the shoreline smiled as she passed.
I smiled back. Farther out now, the teenagers
splashed in the waves, & as I listened to the pitch

of their voices could tell they weren't teenagers
at all but somewhere in the middle of their lives.

"In Therapy I Make Incremental Progress": The poem is in conversation with & indebted to Chen Chen's poem "Self-Portrait as So Much Potential." The word "dutiful" in the last line plays on his use of the word "beautiful."

"Our Language Loves to Show Off": The title & opening lines borrow from Christopher Kempf's poem "The Flower Explosion."

"So Long": *The Plot Against America* is an HBO miniseries that premiered in early 2020, based on the Philip Roth novel. In December of 2018, pix11.com published the headline "Night sky over New York turns blue after electrical fault at Queens Con Edison power plant." The poem's ending adapts the line *"There was no place in nature we could meet"* from Frank Bidart's "Half-Light."

"Walk Through": The opening lines refer to Jenn Shapland's hybrid memoir *My Autobiography of Carson McCullers.*

"Joy": The poem's title comes from Zadie Smith's essay of the same name, which appears in her collection *Feel Free.* The book's epigraph also comes from this essay; Smith writes that a friend of the novelist Julian Barnes "wrote the line in a letter of condolence, and Julian told it to my husband, who told it to me."

"Daughter": The events of this poem take place in the late fall of 2019; in retrospect, the "unknown virus" infecting the racoons was likely Covid-19.

"No Birds": I highly recommend the live stream of Sapsucker Woods hosted by Cornell Labs at https://www.allaboutbirds.org/cams/cornell-lab-feederwatch/.

"Three Days Before What Would Have Been Your Eightieth

Birthday": The poem is inspired by Wendy Xu's poem "Looking Beneath the Sentence's Wing; 1989."

"Dunes": The italicized phrase "*collude anymore with modes of despair*" comes from Bhanu Kapil's author's note about the poem "Collude," which was originally published in Poem-a-Day by the Academy of American Poets in 2019.

ACKNOWLEDGMENTS

Thank you to the editors of the following publications, where some of these poems first appeared: *The Adroit Journal, The Journal, Memorious,* & *The Yale Review.* "Go Inward" was featured on *The Slowdown* podcast hosted by Ada Limón.

I would like to express my immense gratitude to the many people who helped this book along:

To Catherine Barnett, whose mentorship has meant so much to me, thank you for your incisive edits & for the example you set in poetry. To Gabrielle Calvocoressi's Fine Arts Work Center workshop in the summer of 2019 & Kathleen Ossip's 92Y manuscript class in 2020-2021, thank you for helping me to see this book in new ways. To the incomparable Office Hours crew, in particular Marty Correia, Laura Cresté, Linda Harris Dolan, Sophie Herron, Emily Hockaday, Holly Mitchell, Maddie Mori & Sarah Sala, thank you for your friendship & the generous feedback on many of these poems.

To the friends whose presence in my life has made these poems better, infinite thanks to Kelly Bodkin, Jessica Dell, Candi Deschamps, Lizzie Harris, Suzanne Highland, Mike Homolka, Sam Ingerick, Laura Kirk, Doreen Luckey, Mickela Mallozzi, Amy Meng, Reeba Miller, Betsey Osborne, Maya Popa, Karin Portlock, Ben Purkert, Cat Richardson, Jeannine Sam, Margaret Wilkerson Sexton, Cristina Velez, Kerri Vitolo, Shreya Vora, Allison Wilner & Jenny Xie.

To Zachary Schomburg, whose work I've loved for over a decade, I'm so happy to have your painting serve as the cover for this book. To Martha Rhodes, Ryan Murphy, & the team at Four

Way Books, thank you for your belief in my poems. I feel lucky to be part of this community.

Finally, to my family—Mom, Mike, Christina, Amaia, Pia, & Dad, whom we miss daily—thank you for everything. I love you.

About the Author

JEN LEVITT is the author of *The Off-Season*. Her poems have appeared in *The Adroit Journal, Boston Review, Tin House, The Yale Review* and elsewhere. She lives in New York City and teaches high school students.

PUBLICATION OF THIS BOOK WAS MADE POSSIBLE
BY GRANTS AND DONATIONS. WE ARE ALSO GRATEFUL
TO THOSE INDIVIDUALS WHO PARTICIPATED IN
OUR BUILD A BOOK PROGRAM. THEY ARE:

Anonymous (14), Robert Abrams, Michael Ansara, Kathy
Aponick, Jean Ball, Sally Ball, Clayre Benzadón, Adrian Blevins,
Laurel Blossom, adam bohannon, Betsy Bonner, Patricia
Bottomley, Lee Briccetti, Joel Brouwer, Susan Buttenwieser,
Anthony Cappo, Paul and Brandy Carlson, Mark Conway, Elinor
Cramer, Dan and Karen Clarke, Kwame Dawes, Michael Anna
de Armas, John Del Peschio, Brian Komei Dempster, Rosalynde
Vas Dias, Patrick Donnelly, Lynn Emanuel, Blas Falconer, Jennifer
Franklin, John Gallaher, Reginald Gibbons, Rebecca Kaiser
Gibson, Dorothy Tapper Goldman, Julia Guez, Naomi Guttman
and Jonathan Mead, Forrest Hamer, Luke Hankins, Yona Harvey,
KT Herr, Karen Hildebrand, Carlie Hoffman, Glenna Horton,
Thomas and Autumn Howard, Catherine Hoyser, Elizabeth
Jackson, Linda Susan Jackson, Jessica Jacobs and Nickole Brown,
Lee Jenkins, Elizabeth Kanell, Nancy Kassell, Maeve Kinkead,
Victoria Korth, Brett Lauer and Gretchen Scott, Howard Levy,
Owen Lewis and Susan Ennis, Margaree Little, Sara London
and Dean Albarelli, Tariq Luthun, Myra Malkin, Louise Mathias,
Victoria McCoy, Lupe Mendez, Michael and Nancy Murphy,
Kimberly Nunes, Susan Okie and Walter Weiss, Cathy McArthur
Palermo, Veronica Patterson, Jill Pearlman, Marcia and Chris
Pelletiere, Sam Perkins, Susan Peters and Morgan Driscoll, Maya
Pindyck, Megan Pinto, Kevin Prufer, Martha Rhodes, Paula
Rhodes, Louise Riemer, Peter and Jill Schireson, Rob Schlegel,
Yoana Setzer, Soraya Shalforoosh, Mary Slechta, Diane Souvaine,
Barbara Spark, Catherine Stearns, Jacob Strautmann,

Yerra Sugarman, Arthur Sze and Carol Moldaw, Marjorie and Lew Tesser, Dorothy Thomas, Rushi Vyas, Martha Webster and Robert Fuentes, Rachel Weintraub and Allston James, Abigail Wender, D. Wolff, and Monica Youn.